THE ART OF

HEARING
GOD

PRACTICAL STEPS TO DEEPEN YOUR
SPIRITUAL COMMUNICATION

WRITTEN BY

UCHE N. ONYEABO

TABLE OF CONTENTS

INTRODUCTION

The presence of God is here. Let's begin with a verse from Acts 20:32:

> "And now, brethren, I commend you to God and to the word of His grace, which is able to build you up and give you an inheritance among all those who are sanctified."

First and foremost, I entrust you to God, and then to His word. By doing this, I am placing the responsibility for the outcomes in your life into God's hands, much like transferring the care of a small child to a loving guardian. Through the Apostle Paul, God tells us, "I commend you to God and to the word of His grace." This word is powerful in its own right; it doesn't draw strength from any external source. It has the capacity to uplift you and grant you an inheritance among those who are sanctified.

The word of God possesses a transformative power, capable of elevating you to new heights beyond your previous experiences. As you dedicate yourself, it rewards you with an inheritance —something tangible and evident, showcasing that you have truly encountered God and His word.

My prayer is that God, through His Spirit, will continually help us grasp the immense value of His word in a believer's life. Believing that the Word of God is truly His word is just the beginning; you must also believe in its inherent power to transform lives when embraced. Scripture tells us that although Jesus came to His own, they did not receive Him. But to those who did receive Him, He gave the power to become children of God.

Transformation doesn't happen by default. Saul did not become Paul by accident; there is a divine system that molds individuals in God's kingdom. It doesn't matter how you start; if you are willing to engage with the principles of the kingdom, the Word of God promises to transform you.

We often speak about the power of God's word, but many people haven't been adequately taught to recognize its true value. As John 1:1-3 says:

> "In the beginning was the Word, and the Word was with God, and the Word was God. He was with God in the beginning. Through Him all things were made; without Him, nothing was made that has been made."

This means that possessing the Word gives you the ability to influence everything created by it. When God offers you the Word, He is granting you access to His dominion, the authority that created the heavens and the earth. With this Word, you can navigate life and operate on a level that astonishes even principalities and powers.

While this transformation is not instant, for God is not a magician, it is a gradual process that requires your participation. Step by step, principle by principle, if you truly listen and open your heart to receive, no power can derail your destiny. Focus on what God is offering you; it surpasses everything else in value.

Unseen Realms and Divine Allocations

Imagine if all God gave you were material things like a car, a house, and money. However, His true gifts are far more profound, compelling others to be drawn to your light and the brilliance of your rise. In the Bible, blessings are never merely physical; they are spiritual, rooted in the heavenly realms in Christ.

> "He is like a tree planted by streams of water that yields its fruit in its season, and its leaf does not wither. In all that he does, he prospers."
>
> — PSALM 1:3

> "Therefore everyone who hears these words of mine and puts them into practice is like a wise man who built his house on the rock."
>
> — MATTHEW 7:24

In God's kingdom, we reign through the light we possess.

Unfortunately, many focus solely on visible results, often realizing too late the importance of spiritual foundations. God's system requires that the tree is established before the fruit appears. If you only chase results, you may miss the deeper work God is doing in your life.

The devil, master of the sensory realm, will try to manipulate what is visible to discredit God's work in your life. He might challenge, "If you are favored, where is the proof?" But do not be swayed. The Bible says:

> "While we look not at the things which are seen, but at the things which are unseen, for the things which are seen are temporal, but the things which are unseen are eternal."

We must perceive spiritually, using God's Word as our lens. Our understanding should be rooted in the integrity of God's Word, not in our sensory experiences.

Your current experiences may not fully showcase God's faithfulness. If you rely solely on your experiences, you may perceive gaps in God's promises. You might think there are things God has not done. However, your life is too limited to judge God's integrity. Instead, anchor yourself in His Word, saying, "Lord, my life may lack certain things, but I trust in the integrity of Your Word. You do not fail, even if my experience suggests otherwise."

When you reach this understanding, you thwart Satan's attempts to manipulate you with apparent gaps in your life. He might question, "Where is the money if God is faithful?" or "Where is the anointing if you are a man of God?" You might feel called to be a prophet to the nations, yet no one invites you after a year. Is it true that God's hand isn't working in your life? Where are the Gentiles that should come to your light?

Such doubts can discourage you, making you question your calling or wonder if you are under demonic attack. But God says, "Just listen to Me." If you continue in faith, one day it will feel like a dream. You will wake up to a new dimension of the Spirit and marvel, "What is this?" People will say you came out of nowhere, but God knows better.

Meditate on these truths and fully commit yourself to them. Half-hearted faith will not reveal God's full faithfulness. You must throw yourself entirely into your faith, saying, "If I perish, I perish." This complete surrender proves to God that you rely entirely on Him, and He will reveal His greatness to you.

I commend you to God and to the word of His grace, which is able to build you up. Many believers don't understand why the church is mandated to meet frequently. Even pastors might think weekly fellowships are just for generating resources for the ministry. However, the regular gathering of believers is designed by God's intelligence to build and mature the church.

When we gather, we encounter the Spirit of God and learn His ways. Life will not excuse you for what you do not know. Life treats those who disobey and those who are ignorant in the same way. For example, if I am unaware of a depression at the edge of a stage, it won't excuse me from falling and potentially being harmed. Knowledge can deliver you from such dangers. Similarly, we come together to be exposed to God's ways and to experience His power in our midst.

You cannot present a God you have not experienced. It's one thing to know about God's possibilities in theory, and another to have tasted them in your life. You don't need to experience everything, but as God works in your life, you can testify, "Now I know." Your life becomes a living testimony that God is able.

Distractions can prevent believers from focusing on the ministry of the Word. You might attend church and think you're learning just by sitting, but Satan can steal the Word from careless hearts. You might know scriptures and teachings but lack evidence that they have become spirit and life in you.

Challenge yourself to say, "Lord, I am determined to see Your hand in my life." If you see God's hand in one or two areas, it encourages you to trust Him for more. But if you see no evidence of God's hand, it's hard to maintain faith.

> "All Scripture is God-breathed and is useful for teaching, rebuking, correcting and training in righteousness, so that the servant of God may be thoroughly equipped for every good work."
>
> — 2 TIMOTHY 3:16-17

> "So faith comes from hearing, and hearing through the word of Christ."
>
> — ROMANS 10:17

The Word of God builds us up and gives us our place in His kingdom. It assigns us our roles and domains. For instance, when God calls you into the prophetic, the Word allocates you a position, and you operate with God's backing. No one can stand against you because your position was given by the Spirit as a testimony of your faithfulness to God.

Roaming aimlessly without knowing your spiritual jurisdiction is dangerous. Satan can mimic God's voice and lead you to places where you are not equipped to thrive. You might attempt to prophesy without grace and end up frustrated. Knowing your spiritual allocation helps you focus and grow in your assigned domain.

The Word of God gives us spiritual jurisdictions of power and relevance. As we stay with God, He reveals our place in His plan. Whether in ministry, business, or any other field, God allocates us our roles as we remain faithful.

Nobody starts with a clear ministry consciousness. You begin with a love for God and a desire for His presence. Over time, as you prove faithful, God reveals the specifics of your calling. Your initial focus should be on seeking God, not a title or position. As you mature spiritually, God allocates your domain of influence.

Remain faithful and committed to God, and He will reveal your place of dominion. Don't rush or roam aimlessly. Seek God earnestly and allow Him to guide you to your spiritual jurisdiction. This is how you find true fulfillment and effectiveness in your walk with God.

Declaration of Faith and Spiritual Insight

In the name of Jesus, I declare that my journey toward prosperity and divine purpose is rooted not in material possessions, but in the profound spiritual blessings that God has bestowed upon me. I affirm that my true wealth lies in the eternal treasures of God's kingdom, drawing others to His light through the brilliance of His work in my life.

I proclaim that my life is like a tree planted by streams of water, yielding its fruit in its season. My leaves do not wither, and in all I do, I prosper (Psalm 1:3). I am like the wise man who built his house on the rock, hearing and putting into practice the words of the Lord (Matthew 7:24). My foundation is firmly established in God's Word, and no storm can shake my faith.

I reject the lies of the enemy who tries to discredit God's work in my life by manipulating visible circumstances. I do not focus on the seen but on the unseen, knowing that the unseen is eternal (2 Corinthians 4:18). I trust in the integrity of God's Word over my sensory experiences, declaring that God's faithfulness is constant, even if my current circumstances suggest otherwise.

I trust that God is at work, establishing my spiritual roots before the visible fruits appear. I will not be swayed by temporary challenges or delays. My faith is anchored in God's promises, and I believe that in due time, His plans for my life will manifest powerfully.

Lord, I declare that my life, though it may lack certain things now, is a testimony of Your integrity and faithfulness. I trust in Your Word, which never fails. I know that You are at work in ways I may not yet see, and I stand firm in faith, believing that You will bring Your promises to fruition.

I resist the distractions and doubts that try to divert me from my divine purpose. I declare that my focus is on the ministry of the Word and the power of God. I will not allow the enemy to steal the Word from my heart. I am determined to see God's hand in my life, and I trust that His timing is perfect.

My life is a living testimony of God's goodness. I have tasted and seen His possibilities and miracles. I declare that others will see God's hand in my life and be drawn to Him. I commit to sharing my experiences of God's faithfulness, building others up in faith and hope.

I commit to being faithful to God in all aspects of my life. As I seek Him with all my heart, I trust that He will reveal my place of dominion and influence. I will not rush or roam aimlessly but will wait on the Lord to guide me to my spiritual jurisdiction, where I can serve Him effectively and joyfully.

Lord, I thank You for the spiritual blessings and the profound work You are doing in my life. I pray for the grace to remain humble, faithful, and committed to Your purpose. Reveal to me my place of influence and help me to walk in the fullness of Your calling. May my life continually reflect Your glory and draw others to Your light. In Jesus' name, I pray. Amen.

TWO

Journey to True Riches

There are spiritual jurisdictions that require you to grow into certain dimensions before you can fully occupy them. For instance, if God is calling you into an apostolic ministry, you might start as an evangelist. Over two years, you'll serve as an evangelist, then transition to being a teacher. This journey will feel like a mission, and eventually, you'll settle into your calling. Initially, you may identify as an evangelist in America, but as the apostolic grace emerges, it might cause confusion among other evangelists because what you're doing goes beyond traditional evangelism. You'll start teaching from your experiences and might mistakenly believe others are wrong.

Your perseverance in this training is crucial for reaching your ultimate destination. Place immense value on the Word of God, not just reading it but embracing its transformative power. Consider this: if I were your physical father with a small estate, you might wait for me to pass to inherit it. However, physical possessions can be easily seized by authorities. Conversely, when God grants you a spiritual inheritance, no person or force can take it away. Even if people dislike you, when God gives you a key, it opens doors that cannot be ignored by nations.

> "But those who wait on the Lord shall renew their strength; they shall mount up with wings like eagles, they shall run and not be weary, they shall walk and not faint."
>
> — ISAIAH 40:31

> "Be still before the Lord and wait patiently for him; do not fret when people succeed in their ways, when they carry out their wicked schemes."
>
> — PSALM 37:7

These truths bring peace. Questions about your future, greatness, and family well-being are naturally answered as you follow God's training. Many questions arise because we're impatient. If you stay with God, some questions won't even need to be asked. The nature of your questions reveals the kind of student you are. When you are a diligent student under the Spirit of God, you'll find yourself entering dimensions others are praying for, simply because your heart is aligned with Him.

After prolonged guidance, without rushing or comparing yourself to others, you'll find contentment. Others might move forward with jobs and achievements, but you must not feel like you're wandering aimlessly. God reassures you, saying, "Trust me, my son, for now, understand this one thing." Even if you don't yet know your calling, understand the magnitude of God's love for you. Ask God to help you stay focused, resisting the devil's attempts to make you doubt. In one year, God can establish you with new grace, making people exclaim, "I used to know this person, but they've changed!"

You must have a passion for the Word of God. In this kingdom, there are profound discoveries that God, humanity, and even the forces of hell recognize. These discoveries set you apart. By God's grace, you've been given something precious, and I'm guiding you to understand it. I'm reconstructing your understanding of God and the correct approach to life. The value of what you're receiving may not be immediately apparent, but be patient and watch the transformation.

Let's discuss true riches. This isn't about money but about spiritual wealth. Luke 16:11 says:

> "If you have not been trustworthy in handling worldly wealth, who will trust you with true riches?"

This scripture transformed my life. True riches are committed to you by God based on your faithfulness. Ephesians 3:2-8 speaks of the dispensation of grace given to Paul:

> "If ye have heard of the dispensation of the grace of God which is given me to you-ward: How that by revelation he made known unto me the mystery; (as I wrote afore in few words, Whereby, when ye read, ye may understand my knowledge in the mystery of

18

Christ) Which in other ages was not made known unto the sons of men, as it is now revealed unto his holy apostles and prophets by the Spirit; That the Gentiles should be fellowheirs, and of the same body, and partakers of his promise in Christ by the gospel: Whereof I was made a minister, according to the gift of the grace of God given unto me by the effectual working of his power. Unto me, who am less than the least of all saints, is this grace given, that I should preach among the Gentiles the unsearchable riches of Christ."

This grace allowed Paul to understand mysteries previously hidden. These are the unsearchable riches of Christ. Understanding these spiritual blessings establishes the dominion of the saints on earth. The fullness of this dominion is something we are yet to fully experience.

Paul acknowledged that the unsearchable riches of Christ are profound spiritual truths. May God open your eyes to understand these mysteries. These are the blessings by which the dominion of the saints is established. While prophetic declarations affirm the church's dominion, we have yet to fully grasp it in experience.

May you understand the unsearchable riches of Christ, which go beyond material wealth and business success. May God grant you the wisdom to perceive these spiritual truths. These are the principles of Dominion, the systems allocated for the dominion of the saints. The Bible calls it "true riches." There is a grace that God grants by observing your faithfulness. This grace cannot be obtained merely by fasting, praying, or reading books. God bestows it as a reward for faithfulness, granting you access to a mystery called the unsearchable riches of Christ.

Paul taught extensively about this. He said, "I thank my God; I pray in tongues more than you all," indicating his spiritual diligence. When he spoke of this grace, he acknowledged the profound spiritual investment made in his life. He declared that this grace was given to him, who was less than the least of the saints, to be the custodian of a mystery hidden from those who walked with Jesus.

Paul did not see Jesus in the flesh; he was a persecutor at the time. Yet, God chose him, knocking him off his donkey on the way to Damascus, to allocate space for him in this dispensation. Paul was mandated to be the custodian of this mystery, which he received by revelation. He called it the unsearchable riches of Christ.

I have cried and prayed, asking the Lord to remove useless knowledge from my life and grant me access to light and truths that help men and my generation know Him and walk in His life. This has been my prayer, and it remains so.

When the Lord revealed this to me, I was immensely blessed. I am a student, not ashamed to learn from others. I am a product of many spiritual minds. However, in this specific dealing, God opened me up to understand this mystery.

God imparts knowledge to us in different ways: through the stillness of our spirit, through revelation, and spiritual illumination. There are things I know today that I received directly from God, much like a prophetic word. These unsearchable riches are spiritual blessings that provide an advantage for believers to reign on earth.

Declaration of Spiritual Growth and Faithfulness

In the name of Jesus, I declare that I am on a divine journey, growing into the dimensions God has prepared for me. I understand that my calling may evolve over time, and I embrace each stage of my spiritual development with faith and perseverance.

I acknowledge that spiritual jurisdictions require growth and maturity. As I transition from one role to another, I trust in God's process and timing. I may begin as an evangelist, but I know that God is preparing me for greater apostolic grace. I embrace this journey with humility and dedication.

I place immense value on the Word of God, not merely reading it but allowing it to transform my life. I declare that my spiritual inheritance is secure in Christ, and no person or force can take it away. God's blessings open doors that no one can shut.

I trust in God's perfect timing for my life. I will not be impatient or anxious about my future. I know that as I follow God's training, all my questions and concerns will be answered in His time. My perseverance and diligence in God's Word will lead me to new dimensions of grace and blessing.

I resist the distractions and doubts that try to divert me from my divine purpose. I declare that my focus is on the ministry of the Word and the power of God. I will not allow the enemy to steal the Word from my heart. I am determined to see God's hand in my life, and I trust that His timing is perfect.

My life is a living testimony of God's goodness. I have tasted and seen His possibilities and miracles. I declare that others will see God's hand in my life and be drawn to Him. I commit to sharing my experiences of God's faithfulness, building others up in faith and hope.

I declare that true riches are not measured by worldly wealth but by the spiritual blessings God has entrusted to me. I am faithful in handling worldly wealth, and therefore, God trusts me with true riches. I embrace the grace given to me to understand the unsearchable riches of Christ.

I commit to being faithful with the resources and responsibilities God has given me. I seek to understand the profound spiritual truths that establish the dominion of the saints on earth. I ask God to open my eyes to these mysteries and grant me the wisdom to perceive and apply them in my life.

I declare that God is revealing to me the unsearchable riches of Christ. Like Paul, I seek to understand the mysteries of God's grace and share them with others. I am a diligent student of the Spirit, and I embrace the profound spiritual investments God is making in my life.

Lord, I thank You for the spiritual blessings and the profound work You are doing in my life. I pray for the grace to remain humble, faithful, and committed to Your purpose. Reveal to me my place of influence and help me to walk in the fullness of Your calling. May my life continually reflect Your glory and draw others to Your light. In Jesus' name, I pray. Amen.

THREE

Unlocking True Riches: The

Spiritual Advantage

Without a spiritual advantage, ministry becomes a human pursuit of frustration. Men are not kind enough to allow you to excel without the assistance of the spirit realm. From tribal sentiments to the gates of hell and their manipulations, everything seems against you. You only rise and reign in life to the degree to which you sustain a spiritual advantage.

Consider someone trying to push you. If you have a support system, you will achieve results that seem unfair, but these systems provide an advantage. The Bible tells us that these unsearchable riches were designed by God as a proof of His love and determination to see that the saints reign. They fortify us against the gates of hell.

True riches are spiritual blessings that provide an advantage for the believer to reign on earth and manifest the reality of God's life here. Romans 5:17 says,

> "...They which receive the abundance of grace and the gift of righteousness shall reign in life."

This validates our kingship.

Revelation 5:9-10 states,

> "...Thou hast redeemed us to God by thy blood out of every kindred, tongue, people, and nation, and hast made us kings and priests; and we shall reign on earth."

Jesus is the way, the truth, and the life. No one comes to the Father except through Him. He is the only valid access point into the life of the Spirit. Salvation, as described in Romans 10:8-10, involves confessing with your mouth and believing in your heart that God raised Jesus from the dead.

To be saved is to receive new life, a translation into divine life, known as eternal life. This life is the very essence of God, planted in our human spirit by the Holy Spirit. When we become joined to Christ, we become one spirit with Him, similar to the ancient practice of the salt covenant or the mystery of marriage, where two become one.

The Bible warns us not to separate what God has joined because there are significant spiritual implications. Among the many things that happen to man is that his capacity to comprehend spiritual things is quickened by the ministry of the Holy Spirit. The operation of the Word, the logos, and the Spirit of God begin in your life. You start to learn the ways of God, and the Word of God begins to wash you. Just as you wash clothes, it begins to purify your conscience, and your mind is re-educated. The light drives out the darkness gradually, and through these exercises, conformity and transformation occur.

These things will remain for a very long time in your life. You begin to see grace speaking because grace and peace are multiplied through knowledge. This is a laborious assignment because not everything in your mind is of the devil; some things are correct. God will not reset your mind entirely but will transform it with your permission. It's possible to be transformed slowly —one degree in ten years, if that's how slow you want God to take you.

After ten years, you might find that the level of results that should accrue to a life diligent with God is not showing in your life. God is limited by your yieldedness and alignment. This is what begins to separate believers into different categories. Of course, we must also consider the election of grace —people whom God, by His sovereign counsel, has called into certain offices and dimensions. Usually, God will do an unusual work in them, often beyond their personal yieldedness. They cannot take credit for it; it's an acceleration due to the assignment they have to fulfill.

Some people may operate in the prophetic well before they understand what prophecy is. The only thing you need to do is correct their errors, not pray for new visions. They have been seeing visions; they've just been interpreting them incorrectly. Some people, even at the moment of being born again, start seeing visions immediately. Others come from a background of priesthood or wrong spiritual practices, and these open up spiritual sight.

If you meet a native doctor, he might open your spiritual eyes, and even when you get born again, those eyes won't close again. The only thing that changes is you hand over the lordship of that sight to God. There is a spirit that grants access to spiritual realms, and an exchange happens that you are often unaware of. If you have been granted access through a wrong door, you may not know because it's subtle. After ten years, you might find your soul truly sold to the devil.

When you get born again, it's true that your eyes were opened. The charm may stop you from seeing the demons that oppress you, but the realm of the Spirit remains open to you. These are the things that, when I look at my life, make me get down on my knees and thank God. You don't owe God anything; He has been faithful. These systems are very powerful.

The first of these true riches is called the goodness of God. The goodness of God is the grace released on you that allows for the conviction of wrongs and repentance. It is not something you do by your strength. The fortitude to realize the need for alignment is proof that God has been good to you. This is what the Bible means when it talks about the riches of His goodness. Romans 2:1-4 illustrates this well. The goodness of God leads men to repentance. If you are repentant, it is the goodness of God that has come to you. This is not something you achieve by yourself; it is a kingdom expression, a system of consistent realignment to a greater dimension of God's glory.

Many people misunderstand the goodness of God. When the Bible says, "Surely goodness and mercy shall follow me," it's not just a poetic phrase; it's a deep mystery. If the goodness of God does not go with you, you will see the consequences in the lives of people who lack this grace.

Speaking lies in hypocrisy; having their conscience seared with a hot iron;

1 Timothy 4:2 describes people whose consciences are seared with a hot iron, losing the ability to recognize right from wrong. This is what happens to someone who commits heinous acts without remorse. What such a person needs is the goodness of God to break them down and lead them to repentance.

David understood the goodness of God, which is why he was a man after God's heart. Lucifer did not have this goodness; if he did, he would have repented. It is the goodness of God that allows men to see the need for repentance.

Evangelists should pray for the goodness of God when preparing for crusades, as this will lead people to repentance more effectively than any elegant preaching. The generals of faith understood this and carried it in various measures.

The primary assignment of the goodness of God is to create awareness of the need to realign so that we become better reflectors of His glory. The Bible calls it His goodness, one of the true riches of the kingdom.

Declaration of Spiritual Advantage and Divine Alignment

In the name of Jesus, I declare that I am endowed with a spiritual advantage that elevates my ministry beyond human effort and frustration. I recognize that true success in life and ministry is fortified by the unsearchable riches of Christ, which empower me to rise above opposition and manifest God's kingdom on earth.

I receive the abundance of grace and the gift of righteousness, and I reign in life through Christ Jesus. As stated in Romans 5:17, I affirm my kingship and priesthood in God's kingdom.

I am redeemed by the blood of Jesus and made a king and a priest to reign on earth. I exercise my spiritual authority and manifest the reality of God's life in every area of my existence.

I confess with my mouth and believe in my heart that God raised Jesus from the dead. I am saved and have received new life, a translation into divine life, known as eternal life.

This life is the very essence of God, planted in my spirit by the Holy Spirit.

As I am joined to Christ, I become one spirit with Him. I embrace the profound union with Jesus, similar to the mystery of marriage, where two become one. I honor this divine connection and live in alignment with God's will.

My capacity to comprehend spiritual things is quickened by the ministry of the Holy Spirit. The Word of God and the Spirit operate in my life, purifying my conscience and transforming my mind. As light drives out darkness, I experience conformity and transformation into the image of Christ.

Grace and peace are multiplied in my life through the knowledge of God. I diligently seek understanding and revelation, knowing that these true riches are my spiritual inheritance.

I yield myself completely to God's transformative work in my life. I align with His purposes and allow His Spirit to work within me. I refuse to be limited by impatience or comparison with others. I trust God's timing and process, knowing that my faithfulness will lead to extraordinary results.

The goodness of God leads me to repentance and realignment with His will. I am grateful for His grace that convicts me of wrongs and enables me to turn back to Him. This goodness is a true spiritual treasure that keeps me in consistent alignment with God's greater glory.

I walk in the true riches of God's kingdom, which include His goodness, grace, and spiritual blessings. These riches fortify me against the gates of hell and enable me to reign victoriously on earth. I declare that my life reflects the glory and dominion of God, and I am a testimony of His faithfulness and power.

Lord, I thank You for the spiritual advantage and the true riches You have bestowed upon me. I pray for a deeper understanding of Your goodness and grace. Help me to remain yielded and aligned with Your will. May my life continually reflect Your glory and draw others to Your light. In Jesus' name, I pray. Amen.

FOUR

The Riches of God's Wisdom

> "The Lord is not slack concerning his promise, as some men count slackness; but is longsuffering to us-ward, not willing that any should perish, but that all should come to repentance."
>
> — 2 PETER 3:9

God's patience and willingness to save are boundless. He sees our loved ones, aware that their current paths cannot reflect His goodness. It was God's goodness that brought you to this book, not mere coincidence or recommendation. Through His teachings, He seeks to draw you towards salvation, enabling you to align your life with His will and experience His glory.

God's goodness serves as a spiritual advantage, guiding us to realign ourselves so that His light shines brightly through our lives. When people witness the transformation in us, they can see the true wealth of God's goodness. It's not merely about favor or miracles but the profound change and alignment with His purpose. When faced with stubborn or rebellious individuals, the key is intercession for a divine encounter with God's goodness.

A touching testimony illustrates this point. A family, burdened by financial struggles, faced additional trouble when a young boy and his friend took a car and caused an accident. Despite the family's hardships, the boy showed no remorse. Such a lack of repentance signifies the absence of God's goodness. Similarly, hardened criminals who show no guilt for their actions desperately need an encounter with God's goodness.

"Get wisdom, get understanding: forget it not; neither decline from the words of my mouth. Forsake her not, and she shall preserve thee: love her, and she shall keep thee. Wisdom is the principal thing; therefore get wisdom: and with all thy getting get understanding. Exalt her, and she shall promote thee: she shall bring thee to honour, when thou dost embrace her. She shall give to thine head an ornament of grace: a crown of glory shall she deliver to thee."

The second of the unsearchable riches is wisdom. Proverbs emphasizes the importance of wisdom, describing its benefits and urging us to seek it above all else. Wisdom promotes, honors, and bestows grace and glory. A king's crown, symbolizing authority and glory, is given by wisdom.

"Doth not wisdom cry? and understanding put forth her voice? She standeth in the top of high places, by the way in the places of the paths. She crieth at the gates, at the entry of the city, at the coming in at the doors. Unto you, O men, I call; and my voice is to the sons of man. O ye simple, understand wisdom: and, ye fools, be ye of an understanding heart. Hear; for I will speak of excellent things; and the opening of my lips shall be right things. For my mouth shall speak truth; and wickedness is an abomination to my lips. All the words of my mouth are in righteousness; there is nothing froward or perverse in them. They are all plain to him that understandeth, and right to them that find knowledge. Receive my instruction, and not silver; and knowledge rather than choice gold. For wisdom is better than rubies; and all the things that may be desired are not to be compared to it."

—   PROVERBS 8:1-11

Wisdom, like a suitor, presents its benefits, promising that by it, Kings reign and nobles govern justly. It surpasses material wealth, providing durable riches and righteousness. Wisdom is fundamental to creating and sustaining a meaningful life.

"But where shall wisdom be found? and where is the place of understanding? Man knoweth not the price thereof; neither is it found in the land of the living... God understandeth the way thereof, and he knoweth the place thereof... And unto man he said, Behold, the fear of the Lord, that is wisdom; and to depart from evil is understanding."

—   JOB 28:12-28

Wisdom is a divine gift, inaccessible through human effort alone. It requires reverence for God and a departure from evil. When God imparts wisdom, it transforms an ordinary person, enabling them to achieve extraordinary results. Solomon exemplifies this divine wisdom, which brought him unparalleled wealth and honor.

> "Give therefore thy servant an understanding heart to judge thy people, that I may discern between good and bad: for who is able to judge this thy so great a people?... Behold, I have done according to thy words: lo, I have given thee a wise and an understanding heart... And I have also given thee that which thou hast not asked, both riches, and honour: so that there shall not be any among the kings like unto thee all thy days."
>
> — 1 KINGS 3:9-14

Solomon's wisdom exceeded that of all others, making him renowned worldwide. Wisdom produces tangible and sustainable results, elevating men to prominence and enabling them to impact the world positively.

> "And God gave Solomon wisdom and understanding exceeding much, and largeness of heart, even as the sand that is on the seashore."

Job's discourse on wisdom reveals that its true source and location are known only to God. It is not something man can attain through worldly means but a grace bestowed by God. The wisdom of God, when possessed, brings about a life of abundance and fulfillment.

The ability to hear God's voice is another invaluable blessing. Spiritual direction ensures that our actions align with God's will, preventing us from straying into paths of destruction. Many, even prophets, struggle with discerning God's direction, highlighting the importance of seeking this gift earnestly.

> "God understandeth the way thereof, and he knoweth the place thereof."
>
> —   JOB 28:23:

When God imparts wisdom, it leads to a life of extraordinary results and divine alignment. The pursuit of wisdom and the ability to hear God's voice are essential for navigating life's complexities and fulfilling God's purpose for us. Embrace these unsearchable riches, and your life will be a testament to God's glory and wisdom.

Declaration of Divine Patience, Goodness, and Wisdom

I declare that God's patience and willingness to save are boundless. As stated in 2 Peter 3:9, "The Lord is not slack concerning his promise, as some men count slackness; but is longsuffering to us-ward, not willing that any should perish, but that all should come to repentance." I embrace His patience and His desire for my salvation and the salvation of my loved ones. God's goodness brought me to this truth, aligning my life with His will and revealing His glory.

I declare that God's goodness is my spiritual advantage, guiding me to realign my life with His purpose. This goodness is not merely about favor or miracles but about profound change and alignment with His will. As my life is transformed, others will see the true wealth of God's goodness in me. I intercede for those who are stubborn or rebellious, praying for a divine encounter with God's goodness that leads to repentance and transformation.

I declare that I seek wisdom above all else. I exalt wisdom, knowing that it promotes, honors, and bestows grace and glory. Wisdom is the crown of glory on my head, symbolizing my authority and glory in God's kingdom.

I declare that I heed wisdom's call, embracing its benefits which surpass material wealth.

I acknowledge that wisdom is a divine gift, requiring reverence for God and a departure from evil. I seek God's wisdom, knowing it transforms ordinary lives into extraordinary testimonies of His glory.

I declare that like Solomon, I seek an understanding heart to discern between good and bad. God grants me wisdom and understanding, bringing riches and honor as a testament to His blessing.

I declare that I seek the ability to hear God's voice, knowing it is invaluable for aligning my actions with His will. This spiritual direction ensures that I navigate life's complexities and fulfill God's purpose for me.

I embrace the unsearchable riches of God's wisdom and goodness, knowing they lead to a life of extraordinary results and divine alignment. My life is a testament to God's glory and wisdom, and I impact the world positively through His grace. In Jesus' name, Amen.

FIVE

Hearing the Voice of God

One of the unsearchable riches of Christ is the grace to hear the sounds of the Spirit. It's an incredible ability that can be given to men, allowing them to stand firm in their decisions, even when the world advises otherwise. Imagine God telling you to go left while everyone else insists on going right, using common sense as their guide. The true test comes when, after five years, people look at you in amazement, recognizing that you indeed heard God correctly. This ministry, my brothers and sisters, is proof of the transformative power of hearing God.

I'm not one to constantly claim, "God said, God said." I'm cautious, especially now, as many young people have abused that phrase. They might say "God said" simply because they felt something or were under the anointing. However, there are distinct types of communication: the talks of men, the tongues of angels, and the voice of God. Understanding these differences is crucial.

There are times when I hear God speak, and everyone around me knows it. The voice of God comes with a spirit of faith. If you truly hear God, the voice will always be accompanied by faith. Hearing God doesn't leave you idle; it propels you into action. There have been instances where people thought they heard God, only to realize later that it wasn't Him. God is faithful and understands we are students in the school of the Spirit, allowing us to learn and grow.

It's important to understand that God is not always speaking. While He does communicate, it's not a constant stream of words. Just as you are not always talking, neither is God. There have been moments where God has spoken to me, and the resulting grace carried a profound impact.

We must be careful with claiming, "God said." We shouldn't reduce God to the level of a mere man. This doesn't mean we can't hear things; there is the knowing of the Spirit and the witness of the Spirit. These seem like voices, but distinguishing between impulses and God's direct speaking requires deep spiritual discernment. Just because you had a spiritual communication doesn't mean it was God. In the realm of the Spirit, voice is not the only means of communication; light and love also convey messages.

Whenever you claim "God said," seek verification. Every time you say it, you need grace to believe it yourself. Sometimes, you might think you were merely emotional. But upon reflection, you realize it wasn't exactly what you thought.

When God speaks, His power moves in your life. God doesn't care about your current situation; He tells you what He will do, and He will do it. Stand upon your watch and ask, "God, what are You saying in this season?" You need to withdraw from the busyness of life to hear God clearly because many voices and sounds can interrupt His message.

Sometimes, only God can help you discern whether it is truly Him speaking. Most people aren't spiritual enough to reach this realm, so they don't understand. The voice of

God comes with a spirit of faith; after the act is done, you look back and realize it had to be God.

When you hear God, you can sit in the midst of fire and be at peace. People may see the fire and panic, but you rest on the voice of God. Sooner or later, you will need this message. You will carry destinies, and you will need to hear God on their behalf. One day, you will have children and grandchildren, and your spiritual blessing will be tested. As a leader of many, they will rely on your prophetic word.

Pray and ask God, "What is the most accurate spiritual mechanism of communicating Your voice to me? Help me in that area." You may hear but not have trained your hearing. If God speaks to you in dreams, seek clarity. There are dreams that no devil can counterfeit; they are prophetic.

The Hearing Ear and the Seeing Eye are crucial. When Paul was in a storm, an angel appeared and said, "There shall be no loss," and he calmed the people, saying an angel had spoken to him. When you hear God, you can be at peace in any situation.

There are times when you will sit in the midst of uncertainty, but the hearing ear and the seeing eye will provide guidance. An angel appearing to Paul reassured him that there would be no loss, and the storm calmed.

You will need to hear God for yourself and for others. Pray for the ability to discern His voice accurately, as it will be tested. Seek the grace to hear Him clearly and obey His instructions.

Please learn to hear God for your wife and children. One day, God may tell you to move left, and if you rely solely on your degrees and PhD, you might miss His direction. For some of us today, if our parents had heard God, we wouldn't be at this level. We are victims of the lack of hearing God.

Many of our parents were called into ministry but ran away, not hearing God. If they had obeyed, the blessings would have come to us easily. We could have been born again much earlier, but due to their disobedience, our path became harder.

A hearing ear is crucial. Whatever you do with God, if you can't hear Him, it doesn't matter what isn't going well in your life. Hearing God about who to marry, having children, and how to provide for them is vital. Follow His voice; His supplies follow His voice.

Before kings went to war, they inquired of the Lord. We have lost this in our generation, so life often beats us down. For instance, relocating or choosing a place to live should be guided by God. Not every opportunity, like an easy visa interview, means it is from God. The devil can give favor to kill you.

I remember a guy who wanted to go to Italy by arranging a marriage for papers. I don't know where he is now, but he represents someone who did not navigate well.

There are pastors who started well but didn't hear correctly or relied on pride. No matter who you are, if you trivialize God's voice, you will fail. Hearing God as if you are just starting is crucial. Don't let success make you complacent.

Sometimes, well-meaning people advise me to start certain projects or ministries, but I wait to hear from God. The peace of God is a mystery. It can warn you about bad associations or decisions. Peace can indicate whether you are making the right choice.

God's voice takes away wastage from life. Many ministries and finances have gone down because they didn't hear God. Many should not have started churches or organized conferences because God wasn't in it. Happy is the person whose ears can hear God's voice.

Our parents' inability to hear God cost us. There are pastors who are mere shadows of themselves now because they didn't hear God. We have lost destiny helpers because of a lack of wisdom in navigating relationships.

Forget about material things. When you possess spiritual blessings, you can command life. These blessings help you understand how to navigate life effectively. They are true riches that give you an advantage as a believer.

Find a corner and cry to God for the grace to hear Him. This hearing will save your ministry, family, and personal life. The voice of God will help you avoid mistakes and lead you correctly.

We live in an arrogant society where people who don't know where they are going make you feel stupid for staying where God told you to stay. Don't follow others blindly.

After you drop this book, find time to pray and tidy up your ability to hear God. It is crucial for every aspect of life. Ask God to purify your dreams, which can be hijacked by forces. God speaks through various channels, including dreams and visions.

The voice of God will remove wastage from your life. Many have lost loved ones and suffered because they didn't hear God. Pray for a hearing ear and a seeing eye. These encounters and communications from God are vital.

Father, we thank You for this moment. You have shown us the importance of hearing Your voice. Grant us access to a deeper understanding of these truths. May we rise and bring You glory, compelling our generation to know You. We love You and thank You for Your grace upon our lives. In Jesus' name. Amen.

Warfare Section

In the name of Jesus, I declare that I have the grace to hear the sounds of the Spirit. I receive the incredible ability to discern the voice of God, standing firm in my decisions even when the world advises otherwise. I declare that I will follow God's direction, regardless of popular opinion or common sense, knowing that His guidance leads to victory and transformation.

I declare that I will not be misled by emotions or anointing but will seek true spiritual discernment. I recognize the difference between the talks of men, the tongues of angels, and the voice of God. I commit to understanding these distinctions deeply and accurately.

I declare that the voice of God comes with a spirit of faith. When I hear God, I am propelled into action with confidence and assurance. I will not be idle but will act upon His instructions, knowing they carry His power and purpose.

I declare that I will be cautious with claiming, "God said." I will seek verification and grace to believe in His word. I will distinguish between spiritual impulses and God's direct speaking, seeking deep spiritual discernment to know His true voice.

I declare that I will withdraw from the busyness of life to hear God clearly. I will stand upon my watch and ask, "God, what are You saying in this season?" I commit to seeking His guidance in every decision, ensuring His voice is the primary influence in my life.

I declare that I will sit in the midst of fire and be at peace, resting on the voice of God. I will carry destinies and hear God on behalf of others, including my family and future generations. I will seek God's most accurate spiritual mechanism for communicating His voice to me and will train my hearing to discern it clearly.

I declare that I will not rely solely on my degrees or human wisdom but will seek divine direction. I will not be a victim of a lack of hearing God. I will break generational curses of disobedience and spiritual deafness, ensuring that my family walks in divine alignment and blessing.

I declare that I will develop a hearing ear and a seeing eye. I will discern God's voice accurately and obey His instructions. I will seek the grace to hear Him clearly in dreams, visions, and other spiritual communications, ensuring no counterfeit messages mislead me.

I declare that I will not be swayed by the arrogance of society or the opinions of those who do not know God. I will remain steadfast in the place where God has told me to stay, knowing His voice leads to peace and safety.

I declare that God will purify my dreams, protecting them from being hijacked by forces. I will seek clarity in all spiritual communications, ensuring I follow God's true direction.

I declare that the voice of God will remove wastage from my life. I will avoid unnecessary mistakes, losses, and sufferings by hearing and obeying God's guidance. My ministry, family, and personal life will flourish under His divine direction.

Father, in the name of Jesus, I thank You for the grace to hear Your voice. I declare that I will rise in spiritual authority, compelling my generation to know You. I receive deeper understanding and access to the unsearchable riches of Christ, including the ability to hear You clearly. May Your grace and guidance lead me to victory, and may my life bring You glory. Amen.

Made in United States
Troutdale, OR
11/01/2024